ROBINSON CRUSOE

Daniel Defoe

This edition published by Spark Publishing

Spark Publishing
A Division of SparkNotes LLC
120 Fifth Avenue, 8th Floor
New York, NY 10011

Printed and bound in the United States

ISBN 1-58663-487-9

INTRODUCTION: STOPPING TO BUY SPARKNOTES ON A SNOWY EVENING

Whose words these are you *think* you know.
Your paper's due tomorrow, though;
We're glad to see you stopping here
To get some help before you go.

Lost your course? You'll find it here.
Face tests and essays without fear.
Between the words, good grades at stake:
Get great results throughout the year.

Once school bells caused your heart to quake
As teachers circled each mistake.
Use SparkNotes and no longer weep,
Ace every single test you take.

Yes, books are lovely, dark, and deep,
But only what you grasp you keep,
With hours to go before you sleep,
With hours to go before you sleep.

CONTENTS

CONTEXT

DANIEL DEFOE WAS BORN in 1660, in London, and was originally christened Daniel Foe, changing his name around the age of thirty-five to sound more aristocratic. Like his character Robinson Crusoe, Defoe was a third child. His mother and father, James and Mary Foe, were Presbyterian dissenters. James Foe was a middle-class wax and candle merchant. As a boy, Daniel witnessed two of the greatest disasters of the seventeenth century: a recurrence of the plague and the Great Fire of London in 1666. These events may have shaped his fascination with catastrophes and survival in his writing. Defoe attended a respected school in Dorking, where he was an excellent student, but as a Presbyterian, he was forbidden to attend Oxford or Cambridge. He entered a dissenting institution called Morton's Academy and considered becoming a Presbyterian minister. Though he abandoned this plan, his Protestant values endured throughout his life despite discrimination and persecution, and these values are expressed in *Robinson Crusoe*. In 1683, Defoe became a traveling hosiery salesman. Visiting Holland, France, and Spain on business, Defoe developed a taste for travel that lasted throughout his life. His fiction reflects this interest; his characters Moll Flanders and Robinson Crusoe both change their lives by voyaging far from their native England.

Defoe became successful as a merchant, establishing his headquarters in a high-class neighborhood of London. A year after starting up his business, he married an heiress named Mary Tuffley, who brought him the sizeable fortune of 3,700 pounds as dowry. A fervent critic of King James II, Defoe became affiliated with the supporters of the duke of Monmouth, who led a rebellion against the king in 1685. When the rebellion failed, Defoe was essentially forced out of England, and he spent three years in Europe writing tracts against James II. When the king was deposed in the Glorious Revolution of 1688 and replaced by William of Orange, Defoe was able to return to England and to his business. Unfortunately, Defoe did not have the same financial success as previously, and by 1692 he was bankrupt, having accumulated the huge sum of 17,000 pounds in debts. Though he eventually paid off most of the total, he was never again entirely free from debt, and the theme of financial vicissitudes—the wild ups and downs in one's pocketbook—

1

became a prominent theme in his later novels. *Robinson Crusoe* contains many reflections about the value of money.

Around this time, Defoe began to write, partly as a moneymaking venture. One of his first creations was a poem written in 1701, entitled "The True-Born Englishman," which became popular and earned Defoe some celebrity. He also wrote political pamphlets. One of these, *The Shortest Way with Dissenters*, was a satire on persecutors of dissenters and sold well among the ruling Anglican elite until they realized that it was mocking their own practices. As a result, Defoe was publicly pilloried—his hands and wrists locked in a wooden device—in 1703, and jailed in Newgate Prison. During this time his business failed. Released through the intervention of Robert Harley, a Tory minister and Speaker of Parliament, Defoe worked as a publicist, political journalist, and pamphleteer for Harley and other politicians. He also worked as a spy, reveling in aliases and disguises, reflecting his own variable identity as merchant, poet, journalist, and prisoner. This theme of changeable identity would later be expressed in the life of Robinson Crusoe, who becomes merchant, slave, plantation owner, and even unofficial king. In his writing, Defoe often used a pseudonym simply because he enjoyed the effect. He was incredibly wide-ranging and productive as a writer, turning out over 500 books and pamphlets during his life.

Defoe began writing fiction late in life, around the age of sixty. He published his first novel, *Robinson Crusoe*, in 1719, attracting a large middle-class readership. He followed in 1722 with *Moll Flanders*, the story of a tough, streetwise heroine whose fortunes rise and fall dramatically. Both works straddle the border between journalism and fiction. *Robinson Crusoe* was based on the true story of a shipwrecked seaman named Alexander Selkirk and was passed off as history, while *Moll Flanders* included dark prison scenes drawn from Defoe's own experiences in Newgate and interviews with prisoners. His focus on the actual conditions of everyday life and avoidance of the courtly and the heroic made Defoe a revolutionary in English literature and helped define the new genre of the novel. Stylistically, Defoe was a great innovator. Dispensing with the ornate style associated with the upper classes, Defoe used the simple, direct, fact-based style of the middle classes, which became the new standard for the English novel. With *Robinson Crusoe*'s theme of solitary human existence, Defoe paved the way for the central modern theme of alienation and isolation. Defoe died in London on April 24, 1731, of a fatal "lethargy"—an unclear diagnosis that may refer to a stroke.

Plot Overview

ROBINSON CRUSOE IS AN ENGLISHMAN from the town of York in the seventeenth century, the youngest son of a merchant of German origin. Encouraged by his father to study law, Crusoe expresses his wish to go to sea instead. His family is against Crusoe going out to sea, and his father explains that it is better to seek a modest, secure life for oneself. Initially, Robinson is committed to obeying his father, but he eventually succumbs to temptation and embarks on a ship bound for London with a friend. When a storm causes the near deaths of Crusoe and his friend, the friend is dissuaded from sea travel, but Crusoe still goes on to set himself up as merchant on a ship leaving London. This trip is financially successful, and Crusoe plans another, leaving his early profits in the care of a friendly widow. The second voyage does not prove as fortunate: the ship is seized by Moorish pirates, and Crusoe is enslaved to a potentate in the North African town of Sallee. While on a fishing expedition, he and a slave boy break free and sail down the African coast. A kindly Portuguese captain picks them up, buys the slave boy from Crusoe, and takes Crusoe to Brazil. In Brazil, Crusoe establishes himself as a plantation owner and soon becomes successful. Eager for slave labor and its economic advantages, he embarks on a slave-gathering expedition to West Africa but ends up shipwrecked off of the coast of Trinidad.

Crusoe soon learns he is the sole survivor of the expedition and seeks shelter and food for himself. He returns to the wreck's remains twelve times to salvage guns, powder, food, and other items. Onshore, he finds goats he can graze for meat and builds himself a shelter. He erects a cross that he inscribes with the date of his arrival, September 1, 1659, and makes a notch every day in order never to lose track of time. He also keeps a journal of his household activities, noting his attempts to make candles, his lucky discovery of sprouting grain, and his construction of a cellar, among other events. In June 1660, he falls ill and hallucinates that an angel visits, warning him to repent. Drinking tobacco-steeped rum, Crusoe experiences a religious illumination and realizes that God has delivered him from his earlier sins. After recovering, Crusoe makes a survey of the area and discovers he is on an island. He finds a pleasant valley abounding in grapes, where he builds a shady retreat. Crusoe begins to feel more optimistic about being on the island, describing himself as its "king." He trains a pet parrot, takes a goat as a pet, and develops skills in basket weaving, bread making, and pottery. He cuts down an enormous cedar tree and builds a huge canoe from its trunk, but he discovers that he cannot move it to the sea. After building a smaller boat, he rows around the island but nearly perishes when swept away by a powerful current. Reaching shore, he hears his parrot calling his name and is thankful for being saved once again. He spends several years in peace.

One day Crusoe is shocked to discover a man's footprint on the beach. He first assumes the footprint is the devil's, then decides it must belong to one of the cannibals said to live in the region. Terrified, he arms himself and remains on the lookout for cannibals. He also builds an underground cellar in which to herd his goats at night and devises a way to cook underground. One evening he hears gunshots, and the next day he is able to see a ship wrecked on his coast. It is empty when he arrives on the scene to investigate. Crusoe once again thanks Providence for having been saved. Soon afterward, Crusoe discovers that the shore has been strewn with human carnage, apparently the remains of a cannibal feast. He is alarmed and continues to be vigilant. Later Crusoe catches sight of thirty cannibals heading for shore with their victims. One of the victims is killed. Another one, waiting to be slaughtered, suddenly breaks free and runs toward Crusoe's dwelling. Crusoe protects him, killing one of the pursuers and injuring the other, whom the victim finally kills. Well-armed, Crusoe defeats most of the cannibals onshore. The victim vows total submission to Crusoe in gratitude for his liberation. Crusoe names him Friday, to commemorate the day on which his life was saved, and takes him as his servant.

Finding Friday cheerful and intelligent, Crusoe teaches him some English words and some elementary Christian concepts. Friday, in turn, explains that the cannibals are divided into distinct nations and that they only eat their enemies. Friday also informs Crusoe that the cannibals saved the men from the shipwreck Crusoe witnessed earlier, and that those men, Spaniards, are living nearby. Friday expresses a longing to return to his people, and Crusoe is upset at the prospect of losing Friday. Crusoe then entertains the idea of making contact with the Spaniards, and Friday admits that he would rather die than lose Crusoe. The two build a boat to visit the cannibals' land together. Before they have a chance to leave, they are surprised by the arrival of twenty-one cannibals in canoes. The cannibals are holding three victims, one of whom is in European dress. Friday and Crusoe kill most of the cannibals and release the European, a Spaniard. Friday is overjoyed to discover that another of the rescued victims is his father. The four men return to Crusoe's dwelling for food and rest. Crusoe prepares to welcome them into his community permanently. He sends Friday's father and the Spaniard out in a canoe to explore the nearby land. Eight days later, the sight of an approaching English ship alarms Friday. Crusoe is suspicious. Friday and Crusoe watch as eleven men take three captives onshore in a boat. Nine of the men explore the land, leaving two to guard the captives. Friday and Crusoe overpower these men and release the captives, one of whom is the captain of the ship, which has been taken in a mutiny. Shouting to the remaining mutineers from different points, Friday and Crusoe confuse and tire the men by making them run from place to place. Eventually they confront the mutineers, telling them that all may escape with their lives except the ringleader. The men surrender. Crusoe and the captain pretend that the island is an imperial territory and that the governor has spared their lives in order to send them all to England to face justice. Keeping five men as hostages, Crusoe sends the other men out to seize the ship. When the ship is brought in, Crusoe nearly faints.

On December 19, 1686, Crusoe boards the ship to return to England. There, he finds his family is deceased except for two sisters. His widow friend has kept Crusoe's money safe, and after traveling to Lisbon, Crusoe learns from the Portuguese captain that his plantations in Brazil have been highly profitable. He arranges to sell his Brazilian lands. Wary of sea travel, Crusoe attempts to return to England by land but is threatened by bad weather and wild animals in northern Spain. Finally arriving back in England, Crusoe receives word that the sale of his plantations has been completed and that he has made a considerable fortune. After donating a portion to the widow and his sisters, Crusoe is restless and considers returning to Brazil, but he is dissuaded by the thought that he would have to become Catholic. He marries, and his wife dies. Crusoe finally departs for the East Indies as a trader in 1694. He revisits his island, finding that the Spaniards are governing it well and that it has become a prosperous colony.

CHARACTER LIST

Robinson Crusoe The novel's protagonist and narrator. Crusoe begins the novel as a young middle-class man in York in search of a career. He father recommends the law, but Crusoe yearns for a life at sea, and his subsequent rebellion and decision to become a merchant is the starting point for the whole adventure that follows. His vague but recurring feelings of guilt over his disobedience color the first part of the first half of the story and show us how deep Crusoe's religious fear is. Crusoe is steady and plodding in everything he does, and his perseverance ensures his survival through storms, enslavement, and a twenty-eight-year isolation on a desert island.

Friday A twenty-six-year-old Caribbean native and cannibal who converts to Protestantism under Crusoe's tutelage. Friday becomes Crusoe's servant after Crusoe saves his life when Friday is about to be eaten by other cannibals. Friday never appears to resist or resent his new servitude, and he may sincerely view it as appropriate compensation for having his life saved. But whatever Friday's response may be, his servitude has become a symbol of imperialist oppression throughout the modern world. Friday's overall charisma works against the emotional deadness that many readers find in Crusoe.

The Portuguese captain The sea captain who picks up Crusoe and the slave boy Xury from their boat after they escape from their Moorish captors and float down the African coast. The Portuguese captain takes Crusoe to Brazil and thus inaugurates Crusoe's new life as plantation owner. The Portuguese captain is never named—unlike Xury, for example—and his anonymity suggests a certain uninteresting blandness in his role in the novel. He is polite, personable, and extremely generous to Crusoe, buying the animal skins and the

7

slave boy from Crusoe at well over market value. He is loyal as well, taking care of Crusoe's Brazilian investments even after a twenty-eight-year absence. His role in Crusoe's life is crucial, since he both arranges for Crusoe's new career as a plantation owner and helps Crusoe cash in on the profits later.

The Spaniard One of the men from the Spanish ship that is wrecked off Crusoe's island, and whose crew is rescued by the cannibals and taken to a neighboring island. The Spaniard is doomed to be eaten as a ritual victim of the cannibals when Crusoe saves him. In exchange, he becomes a new "subject" in Crusoe's "kingdom," at least according to Crusoe. The Spaniard is never fleshed out much as a character in Crusoe's narrative, an example of the odd impersonal attitude often notable in Crusoe.

Xury A nonwhite (Arab or black) slave boy only briefly introduced during the period of Crusoe's enslavement in Sallee. When Crusoe escapes with two other slaves in a boat, he forces one to swim to shore but keeps Xury on board, showing a certain trust toward the boy. Xury never betrays that trust. Nevertheless, when the Portuguese captain eventually picks them up, Crusoe sells Xury to the captain. Xury's sale shows us the racist double standards sometimes apparent in Crusoe's behavior.

The widow Appearing briefly, but on two separate occasions in the novel, the widow keeps Crusoe's 200 pounds safe in England throughout all his thirty-five years of journeying. She returns it loyally to Crusoe upon his return to England and, like the Portuguese captain and Friday, reminds us of the goodwill and trustworthiness of which humans can be capable, whether European or not.

ANALYSIS OF MAJOR CHARACTERS

While he is no flashy hero or grand epic adventurer, Robinson Crusoe displays character traits that have won him the approval of generations of readers. His perseverance in spending months making a canoe, and in practicing pottery making until he gets it right, is praiseworthy. Additionally, his resourcefulness in building a home, dairy, grape arbor, country house, and goat stable from practically nothing is clearly remarkable. The Swiss philosopher Jean-Jacques Rousseau applauded Crusoe's do-it-yourself independence, and in his book on education, *Emile*, he recommends that children be taught to imitate Crusoe's hands-on approach to life. Crusoe's business instincts are just as considerable as his survival instincts: he manages to make a fortune in Brazil despite a twenty-eight-year absence and even leaves his island with a nice collection of gold. Moreover, Crusoe is never interested in portraying himself as a hero in his own narration. He does not boast of his courage in quelling the mutiny, and he is always ready to admit unheroic feelings of fear or panic, as when he finds the footprint on the beach. Crusoe prefers to depict himself as an ordinary sensible man, never as an exceptional hero.

But Crusoe's admirable qualities must be weighed against the flaws in his character. Crusoe seems incapable of deep feelings, as shown by his cold account of leaving his family—he worries about the religious consequences of disobeying his father, but never displays any emotion about leaving. Though he is generous toward people, as when he gives gifts to his sisters and the captain, Crusoe reveals very little tender or sincere affection in his dealings with them. When Crusoe tells us that he has gotten married and that his wife has died all within the same sentence, his indifference to her seems almost cruel. Moreover, as an individual personality, Crusoe is rather dull. His precise and deadpan style of narration works well for recounting the process of canoe building, but it tends to drain the excitement from events that should be thrilling. Action-packed scenes like the conquest of the cannibals become quite humdrum when Crusoe narrates them, giving us a detailed inventory of the cannibals in list form, for example. His insistence on dating events makes sense to a point, but it ultimately ends up seeming obsessive and irrelevant when he tells us the date on which he grinds his tools but neglects to tell us the date of a very important event like meeting Friday. Perhaps his impulse to record facts carefully is not a survival skill, but an irritating sign of his neurosis.

Finally, while not boasting of heroism, Crusoe is nonetheless very interested in possessions, power, and prestige. When he first calls himself king of the island it seems jocund, but when he describes the Spaniard as his subject we must take his royal delusion seriously, since it seems he really does consider himself king. His teaching Friday to call him "Master," even before teaching him the words for "yes" or "no," seems obnoxious even under the racist standards of the day, as if Crusoe needs to hear the ego-boosting word spoken as soon as possible. Overall, Crusoe's virtues tend to be private: his industry, resourcefulness, and solitary courage make him an exemplary individual. But his vices are social, and his urge to subjugate others is highly objectionable. In bringing both sides together into one complex character, Defoe gives us a fascinating glimpse into the successes, failures, and contradictions of modern man.

FRIDAY

Probably the first nonwhite character to be given a realistic, individualized, and humane portrayal in the English novel, Friday has a huge literary and cultural importance. If Crusoe represents the first colonial mind in fiction, then Friday represents not just a Caribbean tribesman, but all the natives of America, Asia, and Africa who would later be oppressed in the age of European imperialism. At the moment when Crusoe teaches Friday to call him "Master" Friday becomes an enduring political symbol of racial injustice in a modern world critical of imperialist expansion. Recent rewritings of the Crusoe story, like J. M. Coetzee's *Foe* and Michel Tournier's *Friday,* emphasize the sad consequences of Crusoe's failure to understand Friday and suggest how the tale might be told very differently from the native's perspective.

Aside from his importance to our culture, Friday is a key figure within the context of the novel. In many ways he is the most vibrant character in *Robinson Crusoe,* much more charismatic and colorful than his master. Indeed, Defoe at times underscores the contrast between Crusoe's and Friday's personalities, as when Friday, in his joyful reunion with his father, exhibits far more emotion toward his family than Crusoe. Whereas Crusoe never mentions missing his family or dreams about the happiness of seeing them again, Friday jumps and sings for joy when he meets his father, and this emotional display makes us see what is missing from Crusoe's stodgy heart. Friday's expression of loyalty in asking Crusoe to kill him rather than leave him is more heartfelt than anything Crusoe ever says or does. Friday's sincere questions to Crusoe about the devil, which Crusoe answers only indirectly and hesitantly, leave us wondering whether Crusoe's knowledge of Christianity is superficial and sketchy in contrast to Friday's full understanding of his own god Benamuckee. In short, Friday's exuberance and emotional directness often point out the wooden conventionality of Crusoe's personality.

Despite Friday's subjugation, however, Crusoe appreciates Friday much more than he would a mere servant. Crusoe does not seem to value intimacy with humans much, but he does say that he loves Friday, which is a remarkable disclosure. It is the only time Crusoe makes such an admission in the novel, since he never expresses love for his parents, brothers, sisters, or even his wife. The mere fact that an Englishman confesses more love for an illiterate Caribbean ex-cannibal than for his own family suggests the appeal of Friday's personality. Crusoe may bring Friday Christianity and clothing, but Friday brings Crusoe emotional warmth and a vitality of spirit that Crusoe's own European heart lacks.

THE PORTUGUESE CAPTAIN

The Portuguese captain is presented more fully than any other European in the novel besides Crusoe, more vividly portrayed than Crusoe's widow friend or his family members. He appears in the narrative at two very important junctures in Crusoe's life. First, it is the Portuguese captain who picks up Crusoe after the escape from the Moors and takes him to Brazil, where Crusoe establishes himself as a plantation owner. Twenty-eight years later, it is again the Portuguese captain who informs Crusoe that his Brazilian investments are secure, and who arranges the sale of the plantation and the forwarding of the proceeds to Crusoe. In both cases, the Portuguese captain is the agent of Crusoe's extreme good fortune. In this sense, he represents the benefits of social connections. If the captain had not been located in Lisbon, Crusoe never would have cashed in on his Brazilian holdings. This assistance from social contacts contradicts the theme of solitary enterprise that the novel seems to endorse. Despite Crusoe's hard individual labor on the island, it is actually *another human being*—and not his own resourcefulness—that makes Crusoe wealthy in the end. Yet it is doubtful whether this insight occurs to Crusoe, despite his obvious gratitude toward the captain.

Moreover, the Portuguese captain is associated with a wide array of virtues. He is honest, informing Crusoe of the money he has borrowed against Crusoe's investments, and repaying a part of it immediately even though it is financially difficult for him to do so. He is loyal, honoring his duties toward Crusoe even after twenty-eight years. Finally, he is extremely generous, paying Crusoe more than market value for the animal skins and slave boy after picking Crusoe up at sea, and giving Crusoe handsome gifts when leaving Brazil. All these virtues make the captain a paragon of human excellence, and they make us wonder why Defoe includes such a character in the novel. In some ways, the captain's goodness makes him the moral counterpart of Friday, since the European seaman and the Caribbean cannibal mirror each other in benevolence and devotion to Crusoe. The captain's goodness thus makes it impossible for us to make oversimplified oppositions between a morally bankrupt Europe on the one hand, and innocent noble savages on the other.

THEMES, MOTIFS & SYMBOLS

THEMES

Themes are the fundamental and often universal ideas explored in a literary work.

THE AMBIVALENCE OF MASTERY

Crusoe's success in mastering his situation, overcoming his obstacles, and controlling his environment shows the condition of mastery in a positive light, at least at the beginning of the novel. Crusoe lands in an inhospitable environment and makes it his home. His taming and domestication of wild goats and parrots with Crusoe as their master illustrates his newfound control. Moreover, Crusoe's mastery over nature makes him a master of his fate and of himself. Early in the novel, he frequently blames himself for disobeying his father's advice or blames the destiny that drove him to sea. But in the later part of the novel, Crusoe stops viewing himself as a passive victim and strikes a new note of self-determination. In building a home for himself on the island, he finds that he is master of his life—he suffers a hard fate and still finds prosperity.

But this theme of mastery becomes more complex and less positive after Friday's arrival, when the idea of mastery comes to apply more to unfair relationships between humans. In Chapter XXIII, Crusoe teaches Friday the word "[m]aster" even before teaching him "yes" and "no," and indeed he lets him "know that was to be [Crusoe's] name." Crusoe never entertains the idea of considering Friday a friend or equal—for some reason, superiority comes instinctively to him. We further question Crusoe's right to be called "[m]aster" when he later refers to himself as "king" over the natives and Europeans, who are his "subjects." In short, while Crusoe seems praiseworthy in mastering his fate, the praiseworthiness of his mastery over his fellow humans is more doubtful. Defoe explores the link between the two in his depiction of the colonial mind.

13

THE NECESSITY OF REPENTANCE

Crusoe's experiences constitute not simply an adventure story in which thrilling things happen, but also a moral tale illustrating the right and wrong ways to live one's life. This moral and religious dimension of the tale is indicated in the Preface, which states that Crusoe's story is being published to instruct others in God's wisdom, and one vital part of this wisdom is the importance of repenting one's sins. While it is important to be grateful for God's miracles, as Crusoe is when his grain sprouts, it is not enough simply to express gratitude or even to pray to God, as Crusoe does several times with few results. Crusoe needs repentance most, as he learns from the fiery angelic figure that comes to him during a feverish hallucination and says, "Seeing all these things have not brought thee to repentance, now thou shalt die." Crusoe believes that his major sin is his rebellious behavior toward his father, which he refers to as his "original sin," akin to Adam and Eve's first disobedience of God. This biblical reference also suggests that Crusoe's exile from civilization represents Adam and Eve's expulsion from Eden.

For Crusoe, repentance consists of acknowledging his wretchedness and his absolute dependence on the Lord. This admission marks a turning point in Crusoe's spiritual consciousness, and is almost a born-again experience for him. After repentance, he complains much less about his sad fate and views the island more positively. Later, when Crusoe is rescued and his fortune restored, he compares himself to Job, who also regained divine favor. Ironically, this view of the necessity of repentance ends up justifying sin: Crusoe may never have learned to repent if he had never sinfully disobeyed his father in the first place. Thus, as powerful as the theme of repentance is in the novel, it is nevertheless complex and ambiguous.

THE IMPORTANCE OF SELF-AWARENESS

Crusoe's arrival on the island does not make him revert to a brute existence controlled by animal instincts, and, unlike animals, he remains conscious of himself at all times. Indeed, his island existence actually deepens his self-awareness as he withdraws from the external social world and turns inward. The idea that the individual must keep a careful reckoning of the state of his own soul is a key point in the Presbyterian doctrine that Defoe took seriously all his life. We see that in his normal day-to-day activities, Crusoe keeps accounts of himself enthusiastically and in various ways. For example, it is significant that Crusoe's makeshift calendar does not simply mark the passing of days, but instead more egocentrically marks the days he has spent on the island: it is about him, a sort of self-conscious or autobiographical calendar with him at its center. Similarly, Crusoe obsessively keeps a journal to record his daily activities, even when they amount to nothing more than finding a few pieces of wood on the beach or waiting inside while it rains. Crusoe feels the importance of staying aware of his situation at all times. We can also sense Crusoe's impulse toward self-awareness in the fact that he teaches his parrot to say the words, "Poor Robin Crusoe. . . . Where have you been?" This sort of self-examining thought is natural for anyone alone on a desert island, but it is given a strange intensity when we recall that Crusoe has spent months teaching the bird to say it back to him. Crusoe teaches nature itself to voice his own self-awareness.

MOTIFS

> *Motifs are recurring structures, contrasts, or literary devices that can help to develop and inform the text's major themes.*

COUNTING AND MEASURING

Crusoe is a careful note-taker whenever numbers and quantities are involved. He does not simply tell us that his hedge encloses a large space, but informs us with a surveyor's precision that the space is "150 yards in length, and 100 yards in breadth." He tells us not simply that he spends a long time making his canoe in Chapter XVI, but that it takes precisely twenty days to fell the tree and fourteen to remove the branches. It is not just an immense tree, but is "five foot ten inches in diameter at the lower part . . . and four foot eleven inches diameter at the end of twenty-two foot." Furthermore, time is measured with similar exactitude, as Crusoe's journal shows. We may often wonder why Crusoe feels it useful to record that it did not rain on December 26, but for him the necessity of counting out each day is never questioned. All these examples of counting and measuring underscore Crusoe's practical, businesslike character and his hands-on approach to life. But Defoe sometimes hints at the futility of Crusoe's measuring—as when the carefully measured canoe cannot reach water or when his obsessively kept calendar is thrown off by a day of oversleeping. Defoe may be subtly poking fun at the urge to quantify, showing us that, in the end, everything Crusoe counts never really adds up to much and does not save him from isolation.

EATING

One of Crusoe's first concerns after his shipwreck is his food supply. Even while he is still wet from the sea in Chapter V, he frets about not having "anything to eat or drink to comfort me." He soon provides himself with food, and indeed each new edible item marks a new stage in his mastery of the island, so that his food supply becomes a symbol of his survival. His securing of goat meat staves off immediate starvation, and his discovery of grain is viewed as a miracle, like manna from heaven. His cultivation of raisins, almost a luxury food for Crusoe, marks a new comfortable period in his island existence. In a way, these images of eating convey Crusoe's ability to integrate the island into his life, just as food is integrated into the body to let the organism grow and prosper. But no sooner does Crusoe master the art of eating than he begins to fear being eaten himself. The cannibals transform Crusoe from the consumer into a potential object to be consumed. Life for Crusoe always illustrates this *eat or be eaten* philosophy, since even back in Europe he is threatened by man-eating wolves. Eating is an image of existence itself, just as being eaten signifies death for Crusoe.

ORDEALS AT SEA

Crusoe's encounters with water in the novel are often associated not simply with hardship, but with a kind of symbolic ordeal, or test of character. First, the storm off the coast of Yarmouth frightens Crusoe's friend away from a life at sea, but does not deter Crusoe. Then, in his first trading voyage, he proves himself a capable merchant, and in his second one, he shows he is able to survive enslavement. His escape from his Moorish master and his successful encounter with the Africans both occur at sea. Most significantly, Crusoe survives his shipwreck after a lengthy immersion in water. But the sea remains a source of danger and fear even later, when the cannibals arrive in canoes. The Spanish shipwreck reminds Crusoe of the destructive power of water and of his own good fortune in surviving it. All the life-testing water imagery in the novel has subtle associations with the rite of baptism, by which Christians prove their faith and enter a new life saved by Christ.

SYMBOLS

Symbols are objects, characters, figures, or colors used to represent abstract ideas or concepts.

THE FOOTPRINT

Crusoe's shocking discovery of a single footprint on the sand in Chapter XVIII is one of the most famous moments in the novel, and it symbolizes our hero's conflicted feelings about human companionship. Crusoe has earlier confessed how much he misses companionship, yet the evidence of a man on his island sends him into a panic. Immediately he interprets the footprint negatively, as the print of the devil or of an aggressor. He never for a moment entertains hope that it could belong to an angel or another European who could rescue or befriend him. This instinctively negative and fearful attitude toward others makes us consider the possibility that Crusoe may not want to return to human society after all, and that the isolation he is experiencing may actually be his ideal state.

THE CROSS

Concerned that he will "lose [his] reckoning of time" in Chapter VII, Crusoe marks the passing of days "with [his] knife upon a large post, in capital letters, and making it into a great cross . . . set[s] it up on the shore where [he] first landed. . . ." The large size and capital letters show us how important this cross is to Crusoe as a timekeeping device and thus also as a way of relating himself to the larger social world where dates and calendars still matter. But the cross is also a symbol of his own new existence on the island, just as the Christian cross is a symbol of the Christian's new life in Christ after baptism, an immersion in water like Crusoe's shipwreck experience. Yet Crusoe's large cross seems somewhat blasphemous in making no reference to Christ. Instead, it is a memorial to Crusoe himself, underscoring how completely he has become the center of his own life.

CRUSOE'S BOWER

On a scouting tour around the island, Crusoe discovers a delightful valley in which he decides to build a country retreat or "bower" in Chapter XII. This bower contrasts sharply with Crusoe's first residence, since it is built not for the practical purpose of shelter or storage, but simply for pleasure: "because I was so enamoured of the place." Crusoe is no longer focused solely on survival, which by this point in the novel is more or less secure. Now, for the first time since his arrival, he thinks in terms of "pleasantness." Thus, the bower symbolizes a radical improvement in Crusoe's attitude toward his time on the island. Island life is no longer necessarily a disaster to suffer through, but may be an opportunity for enjoyment—just as, for the Presbyterian, life may be enjoyed only after hard work has been finished and repentance achieved.

Summary & Analysis

Preface & Chapters I–III

Summary: Preface

An unnamed editor explains his reasons for offering us the narrative we are about to read. He does not mention the name or story of Robinson Crusoe explicitly but, rather, describes the narrative as a "private man's adventures in the world" and focuses on its realism when he calls it a "just history of fact." He claims it is modest and serious, and that it has an instructive value, teaching us to honor "the wisdom of Providence." Thus, the editor asserts he is doing a great service to the world in publishing Crusoe's tale.

Summary: Chapter I — *I Go to Sea*

I was born in the year 1632, in the city of York, of a good family, though not of that country, my father being a foreigner.... (See QUOTATIONS, p. 45)

A man named Robinson Crusoe records his own life story, beginning with his birth in 1632 in the English city of York. Crusoe's father was a German, originally named Kreutznaer. Crusoe is the youngest of three brothers, the eldest being a soldier and the second one having vanished mysteriously. As the youngest son in the family, Crusoe is expected to inherit little, and, as a result, his father encourages him to take up the law. But Crusoe's inclination is to go to sea. His family strongly opposes this idea, and his father gives him a stern lecture on the value of accepting a middle station in life. Crusoe resolves to follow his father's advice. But when one of his friends embarks for London, Crusoe succumbs to temptation and boards the ship on September 1, 1651. A storm develops. Near Yarmouth the weather is so bad that Crusoe fears for his life and prays to God for deliverance. The ship nearly founders, but all are saved. Crusoe sees this ordeal as a sign of fate that he should give up sea travel, and his friend's father warns him against setting foot on a ship again, echoing his own father's warning.

SUMMARY: CHAPTER II — *I Am Captured by Pirates*
Crusoe parts with his friend and proceeds to London by land, where he meets a sea captain who proposes that Crusoe accompany him on an upcoming merchant voyage. Writing to his family for investment money, Crusoe sets off with forty pounds worth of trinkets and toys to sell abroad. Crusoe makes a net income of 300 pounds from this trip, and considers it a great success. Taking one hundred pounds with him, and leaving the remaining 200 pounds with a widow whom he trusts, Crusoe sets off on another merchant expedition. This time he is pursued by Moorish pirates off the coast of Sallee in North Africa. His ship is overtaken, and Crusoe is enslaved, the only Briton among his Moorish master's slaves. Crusoe is assigned the task of fishing because of his natural skill. One day the slaves' fishing vessel gets lost in fog, and the master installs a compass on board. The master also stores some gunpowder on board in preparation for a shooting party, but the guests do not come. Crusoe waits.

SUMMARY: CHAPTER III —
I Escape from the Sallee Rover
Robinson sets off on a fishing expedition with two other slaves, a man named Ismael and a boy named Xury. Sneaking up behind Ismael, Robinson pushes him into the water. Ismael swims alongside the boat and begs to be taken in. Crusoe pulls a gun on him and tells him to return to shore or else be killed. Crusoe then asks Xury whether he will accompany him and serve him faithfully, and Xury agrees. By evening, Crusoe calculates they have sailed 150 miles south of Sallee. They see wild creatures onshore that Crusoe recognizes as lions. Crusoe shoots one dead, and he and Xury skin it. They proceed southward toward what Crusoe believes are the Cape Verde or Canary Islands. They see naked black people onshore, and they fear them until the natives offer them food. When the Africans witness Crusoe shooting a leopard, they are impressed, and they offer the skin to Crusoe. Unsure where to head, Crusoe is surprised by a European ship in the distance. The ship picks up Xury and Crusoe, and its kind Portuguese captain offers to take them to Brazil. The captain buys Crusoe's boat as well as Xury.

ANALYSIS: PREFACE & CHAPTERS I–III
These chapters introduce us to Crusoe's particular style of narration, which revolutionized the English novel: he speaks openly and

intimately, with none of the grandiose rhetorical effects notable in earlier ages of English literary history. In telling us frankly how much profit he makes from his first merchant venture, and in acknowledging his inner struggle about obeying his father or following his desire to go to sea, Crusoe addresses us as if we are his close and trusted friends. He is also an exceedingly practical and fact-oriented narrator, as the editor emphasizes in calling the narration a "just history of fact." Crusoe is fixated on precise details, telling us the exact day he set off on his voyage and the number of miles south of Sallee he is. His feelings are less fully narrated, though he does relate his anguish at disobeying his father. Crusoe also shows his basic kindness and humanity in sparing the life of Ismael, though it is clear that this act is a minor detail for him. His focus on facts, actions, and details helps mark the beginning of the novelistic form in English literature.

Crusoe's narrative is not just an adventure story about storms and pirates, but also what in religious literature is called an *exemplary tale*: a tale told for purposes of moral and religious instruction. In the Preface, the editor explicitly tells us that this novel will teach us to honor "the wisdom of Providence." We are meant to learn something spiritually useful when reading this story. Crusoe underscores this spiritual aspect by focusing on his wickedness in disobeying his father's orders, and the punishments that come upon him for doing so. In Chapter II he refers to the "evil influence which carried me first away from my father's house," and the word "evil" is important: this choice is not just a foolish decision, but one made with a morally wicked influence. Moreover, the evil curiously makes Crusoe its passive victim, introducing another central aspect of Robinson's story—his own passivity. Crusoe's place as the rebellious younger son in the family, resembling the Prodigal Son in the Bible, enhances the religious side of Crusoe's story.

The idea of foreignness is introduced as an important foreshadowing of Crusoe's later long existence as a castaway in an alien land. Interestingly, despite the story's beginning in Hull and London, Crusoe does not focus much attention on any Englishmen in his narrative. The friend who tempts him on board the ship is not named, and Crusoe shows no real affection for him. Not even Crusoe's family members are named. The English simply do not appear to excite his interest. By contrast, Crusoe is quick to tell us the names of the other slaves, Ismael and Xury, on the Moorish fishing boat. The Portuguese captain is not named, but he is described with much more vividness than the first English captain. Crusoe reveals a basic predisposition toward foreigners that underscores his early inclination to go to sea and leave England. As the son of a foreigner—his father's name was Kreutznaer—this roaming may be his fate. Perhaps like Odysseus in *The Odyssey*, he is simply destined by nature to leave home.

CHAPTERS IV–VII

SUMMARY: CHAPTER IV — *I Become a Brazilian Planter*
After a voyage of twenty-two days, Crusoe lands in Brazil, accepting many farewell gifts from the Portuguese captain. After meeting his Anglo-Brazilian neighbor, he conceives a plan to become a tobacco planter. For two years Crusoe earns only enough on which to subsist, but in the third year he begins to do well and, in retrospect, misses the labor potential of the slave boy Xury whom he sold. Having told the Portuguese captain of his 200 pounds left in England, the captain arranges to have one hundred pounds sent to Crusoe in Brazil, along with many gifts besides. After receiving what the captain sent, Crusoe feels quite well off. Eager for slave labor to extend his business further, he agrees to an acquaintance's plan to sail to Guinea for black slaves, in exchange for his own share of the slaves.

SUMMARY: CHAPTER V —
I Go on Board in an Evil Hour
After writing a will leaving half his possessions to the Portuguese captain, Crusoe sets sail for Guinea on September 1, 1659 with a cargo of trinkets with which to buy slaves. Sailing up the South American coast, the ship encounters a storm, and two men are lost. Crusoe fears for his life. Reaching the Caribbean, the ship is shaken by yet another storm that drives the ship onto the sand, breaking the rudder. The ship is clearly doomed, and the crew climbs into boats to make for shore. Crusoe loses sight of his mates when all are swept away by an immense wave. Finally Crusoe makes it to shore, where he immediately prays to God in gratitude. He never sees a sign of another living crewmember. After drinking some fresh water and finding a tree in which to sleep, Crusoe spends his first night on the island.

Summary: Chapter VI —
I Furnish Myself with Many Things

> *"O drug!" said I aloud, "what art thou good for?"*

Awakening the next morning refreshed, Crusoe goes down to the shore to explore the remains of the ship. Swimming around it, he finds it impossible to climb aboard until he finds a chain hanging, by which he pulls himself up. Crusoe conceives the idea of building a raft out of broken lumber, on which he loads provisions of bread, rice, goat meat, cheese, and other foods. He also finds clothes, arms, and fresh water. He sails his cargo-laden raft into a small cove, where he unloads it. He notices that the land has wildfowl but no other humans. Crusoe returns to the ship twelve times over the following thirteen days. On one of the later trips he finds thirty-six pounds, and he sadly meditates on how worthless the money is to him. After a strong wind that night, he awakens to find the ship's remains gone the next morning.

Summary: Chapter VII - *I Build My Fortress*

Wary of savages, Crusoe decides he must build a dwelling or "fortress," as he calls it. He chooses a spot with a view of the sea, protected from animals and the heat of the sun and near fresh water. He drives wooden stakes into the ground, using them as a frame for walls. Crusoe sleeps securely in the shelter that night. The next day he hauls all of his provisions and supplies inside, and hangs a hammock on which to sleep. He also builds a cellar. During a thunderstorm he suddenly worries about his gunpowder supply, which he separates from the other supplies and stores in the cellar. Crusoe discovers wild goats on the island. He kills one and then sees that it had a kid, which he then kills too. On about his twelfth day on the island, he erects a large cross that he inscribes with the date of his arrival, September 30, 1659. He resolves to cut a notch on the cross to mark every passing day. He also begins a journal in which he records the good and evil aspects of his experience, until he runs out of ink. He keeps watch for passing ships, always disappointed.

Analysis: Chapters IV–VII

The question of whether Crusoe's humanity will survive on the island, or whether he will revert to savagery, is subtly raised in these chapters. His changing relationship to Xury is one example of a test of morality. During his early acquaintance with the boy, Crusoe appears genuinely fond of him, moved by the boy's expression of loyalty and by their solidarity as slaves of the same master. But then, Crusoe, recently a slave himself, coldly sells Xury to the Portuguese captain with no compunction at all. When Crusoe thinks about Xury later, he does not recollect memories of a long-lost acquaintance, but instead laments missing out on the potential for slave labor: he and his planter neighbor "both wanted help, and now I found, more than before, I had done wrong in parting with my boy Xury." We might feel what is "wrong" is not his business decision, but the sale of his supposed friend as a slave for profit. The question of whether morality is socially adaptable or naturally inborn was disputed in seventeenth-century England: the philosopher Thomas Hobbes maintained that men are naturally savages. Crusoe is a case study in the nature of human morals.

Crusoe's sense of religion seems, on the one hand, to develop strongly, but on the other hand, some of his words do raise some doubt about his beliefs. Certainly he appears very devout when his first reaction on reaching dry land after his shipwreck is "to look up and thank God that my life was saved in a case wherein here was some minutes before scarce any room to hope." But, as many have noticed, his comments right after this remark are theologically unsound: "I believe it is impossible to express to the life what the ecstasies and transports of the soul are when it is so saved, as I may say, out of the very grave. . . ." As any devout Christian of Defoe's day would know, the *soul* is eternal, and what Crusoe should instead say is that his bodily life is saved. The remark is thus a bit ignorant even at the moment when he appears to be deeply God-fearing. Later, when he builds a cross on the island and devotes it to *himself* and his time on the island, rather than to Christ, our doubt over his true faith in God grows further.

Crusoe's relation to material possessions is a prominent topic in these chapters. Crusoe repeatedly suggests that his shipwreck is a punishment for his greed for profits and that his pursuit of ever more material wealth has caused his current misery. His biblical prototype Job, another survivor of a disaster at sea, learns from his ordeal to disdain material possessions. Crusoe's survival on the island seems like a rebirth into true Christian spirituality, a chance to live less materially and more religiously. Yet when Crusoe makes not one or two, but *twelve* trips to the ship for salvaged supplies, we wonder how nonmaterialistic he has really become. It is doubtful that in his

solitude he needs "a dozen of good knives and forks." He proudly
entitles one of his chapters *I Furnish Myself with Many Things.*
When he discovers thirty-six pounds in coins on the ship, he first dis-
dains it with Christian high-mindedness, saying, "Oh drug, what art
thou good for," but then he takes the money with him anyway. His
attitude toward possessions seems a major contradiction in his character, and these sorts of contradictions exist throughout the novel.

CHAPTERS VIII–XII

SUMMARY: CHAPTER VIII — *The Journal*

Crusoe makes us privy to the journal that he keeps for a while,
beginning with an entry dated "September 30, 1659," that inaugurates his account of life on the "Island of Despair," as he calls it. He
proceeds to narrate events that have already been narrated: his discovery of the ship's remains, his salvaging of provisions, the storm
that destroys the ship entirely, the construction of his house, and so
on. He notes that he has lost track of which day is Sunday, and he is
thus unable to keep the Sabbath religiously. He records the building
of various pieces of furniture and tools. He tames his first goat.

SUMMARY: CHAPTER IX —
I Throw Away the Husks of Corn

Continuing his journal, Crusoe records his failed attempt to tame
pigeons and his manufacture of candles from goat grease. He tells of
his semimiraculous discovery of barley: having tossed out a few
husks of corn in a shady area, he is astonished to find healthy barley
plants growing there later. He carefully saves the harvest to plant
again and thus is able eventually to supply himself with bread. On
April 16, an earthquake nearly kills him as he is standing in the
entrance to his cellar. After two aftershocks, he is relieved to feel it
end with no damage to his life or property.

SUMMARY: CHAPTER X —
It Blows a Most Dreadful Hurricane

Immediately after the earthquake, a hurricane arrives. Crusoe takes
shelter in his cave, cutting a drain for his house and waiting out the
torrential rains. He is worried by the thought that another earthquake would send the overhanging precipice falling onto his dwelling and resolves to move. But he is distracted from this plan by the

discovery of casks of gunpowder and other remains from the ship that have been driven back to shore by the hurricane. Crusoe spends many days salvaging these remains for more useful items.

SUMMARY: CHAPTER XI —
I Am Very Ill and Frighted
For more than a week of rainy weather, Crusoe is seriously ill with a fever and severe headache. He is almost too weak to get up for water, though he is dying of thirst. He prays to God for mercy. In one of his feverish fits, he hallucinates a vision of a man descending from a black cloud on a great flame. The man brandishes a weapon at Crusoe and tells him that all his suffering has not yet brought him to repentance. Crusoe emerges from the vision to take stock of the many times he has been delivered from death and cries over his ingratitude. He utters his first serious prayer to God, asking for an end to his distress. The next day, Crusoe finds he is beginning to recover, though he is still so weak he can hardly hold his gun. He struggles with thoughts of self-pity followed by self-reproach. Taking some tobacco and rum, his mind is altered and he opens the Bible to read a verse about calling on the Lord in times of trouble, which affects him deeply. He falls into a profound sleep of more than twenty-four hours, which throws off his calendar calculations forever. In the days that follow, Crusoe almost completely recovers and kneels to God in gratitude. He prefers not to eat the wildfowl while sick and instead eats some turtle eggs that he finds. He begins a serious reading of the New Testament and regrets his earlier life. He comes to conceive of his isolation on the island as a kind of deliverance from his former guilty existence.

SUMMARY: CHAPTER XII —
I Take a Survey of the Island
Now, in the month of July, in his tenth month on the island, Crusoe discovers that the rainy season is a very unhealthy time. Having acquiesced in the idea that only Providence controls his deliverance from the island, Crusoe resolves to explore the place thoroughly. He discovers sugarcane and grapes, and is delighted with the beauty of one valley especially. He secretly exults in imagining himself the king and lord of the whole domain. Crusoe lays out grapes to make raisins and carries home a large basket of limes and grapes. He contemplates choosing that site as his new home, then spends the rest of July building a bower in the valley. He notes that his domicile now

houses some cats. He celebrates the passing of one year on the island by fasting all day. Shortly after this occasion, he runs out of ink and discontinues his journal.

ANALYSIS: CHAPTERS VIII–XII

Crusoe's journal provides little interesting new information for us, since most of it narrates previously recounted material. But it does offer insights into Crusoe's character, especially his conception of his own identity. First, he introduces himself as "poor, miserable Robinson Crusoe," which strikes a startling note of self-pity that contradicts the sturdy, resourceful self-image of his narrative. There may be some grandiose posturing in this journal. Moreover, as many have noticed, Crusoe's journal is false in its dating, despite its author's loudly trumpeted concern for absolute accuracy. By Crusoe's own admission, he states that he arrived on the island on the thirtieth of September. His idea of a journal comes only later: "After I had been there about ten or twelve days, it came into my thoughts, that I should lose my reckoning of time for want of books, and pen and ink. . . ." Thus he keeps no journal for the first ten or twelve days. Yet his first journal entry is dated "September 30, 1659," the day of his arrival. Clearly Crusoe likes the idea of using the journal to account for all his time on the island, giving himself an aura of completeness, even if it requires some sneaky bookkeeping to do so. This deception suggests to us that his interest in the hard facts may be less than objective, and may actually be more subjective and self-serving.

The most important psychological development in these chapters is Crusoe's born-again conversion. Crusoe has had many religious moments, sometimes quickly forgotten. One example of this forgetting occurs when he first calls the sprouting corn a miracle, then later attributes it to mere good luck. But during his illness, his turn to religion seems profound and lasting. His hallucination of a wrathful angel figure that threatens him for not repenting his sins is a major event in his emotional life, which up to this point has seemed free from such wild imaginings. When he later takes tobacco-steeped rum and reads a verse of the Bible that tells him to call upon God in times of trouble, he seems deeply affected. Indeed, his loss of a day from his calendar may represent his relinquishment of total control of his life and his acknowledgment of a higher power in charge. When he falls on his knees to thank God for delivering him from his illness, his faith seems sincere. This faith forces him to reevaluate the island itself, which, he tells himself, may not be a place of captivity, but a place of deliverance from his earlier sins. He thus redefines his whole landscape—and his whole life—much more optimistically.

Partly as a result of Crusoe's born-again experience, his attitude toward the island improves dramatically. No longer viewing it as a place of punishment and misery, he starts to see it as his home. Indeed, he now uses the word "home" explicitly in reference to his camp. Significantly, he now notices how beautiful parts of the island are when he explores the terrain after his recovery. He describes the "delicious vale" that he discovers, in which he decides to build a bower. He surveys the area "with a secret kind of pleasure . . . to think that this was all my own, that I was king and lord of all this country indefeasibly and had a right of possession." This attitude shift is extraordinary. He no longer views himself, as he does in his first journal entry, as "poor, miserable Robinson," but is now feeling the pleasure of calling himself king and lord of a delicious vale. Yet his happiness in his island life is short-lived, since only a few pages later he refers to the "unhappy anniversary of my landing," as if forgetting that his landing, in a different perspective, seems cause for rejoicing. Defoe is underscoring the extent to which Crusoe's sense of fate and suffering is not objective, but rather created by his own mind.

CHAPTERS XIII–XVII

SUMMARY: CHAPTER XIII — *I Sow My Grain*

After planting his grain in the dry season when it cannot sprout, Crusoe learns from his mistake, and afterward makes a table of the dry and rainy months to facilitate his farming. He also discovers that the wooden stakes he drove into the ground when building his "bower," or country house, have sprouted and grown. Over the course of several years they grow into a kind of sheltering hedge providing cool shade. Crusoe also teaches himself to make wicker baskets, imitating the basket makers he remembers from his childhood. By this time he lacks only tobacco pipes, glassware, and a kettle.

Summary: Chapter XIV —
I Travel Quite Across the Island
Finally carrying out his earlier wish to survey the island thoroughly, Crusoe proceeds to the western end, where he finds he can make out land in the distance. He concludes it belongs to Spanish America. Crusoe is reluctant to explore it for fear of cannibals. He catches a parrot that he teaches to speak, and discovers a penguin colony. He takes a goat kid as a pet, keeping it in his bower where it nearly starves until Crusoe remembers it. By this point, Crusoe has been on the island two years, and his moments of satisfaction alternate with despairing moods. He continues to read the Bible and is consoled by the verse that tells him God will never forsake him.

Summary: Chapter XV — I Am Very Seldom Idle
Crusoe spends months making a shelf for his abode. During the rainy months he plants his crop of rice and grain but is angered to discover that birds damage it. He shoots several of the birds and hangs them as scarecrows over the plants, and the birds never return. Crusoe finally harvests the grain and slowly learns the complex process of flour grinding and bread making. Determined to make earthenware pots, Crusoe attempts to shape vessels out of clay, failing miserably at first. Eventually he learns to shape, fire, and even glaze his pots. Thinking again of sailing to the mainland, Crusoe returns to the place where the ship's boat has been left upturned by the storm. He tries for weeks to put it right side up but is not strong enough.

Summary: Chapter XVI — I Make Myself a Canoe

"Poor Robin Crusoe! Where are you? Where have you been? How come you here?"
(See QUOTATIONS, p. 47)

Resolving to make a canoe, Crusoe selects and cuts down an enormous cedar. He spends many months hacking off the branches, shaping the exterior, and hollowing out the insides. The result is a far larger canoe than he has ever seen before. He now realizes the mistake of not previously considering its transport, since for him alone it is immovable. He considers building a canal to bring the water to the canoe, but he calculates it would take too long and abandons the idea. By this point, four years have passed. He reflects that all his wants are satisfied, since he already has everything that he can possibly use on his island. He feels gratitude imagining how much worse off he could be now. He also reflects on several calendar coincidences that he finds remarkable: he left his family on the same day he was enslaved by the Moor; he escaped from the ship near Yarmouth on the same day that he escaped from Sallee; and he was born on the same day he was cast ashore on the island. Crusoe undertakes to make himself some new clothing out of animal skins, and he also constructs an umbrella. Building a smaller canoe, he sets out on a tour around the island. He is caught in a dangerous current that threatens to take him out to sea and away from the island forever, and when he is saved he falls to the ground in gratitude. Crusoe hears a voice say his name repeatedly on his return, asking where he has been, and Crusoe discovers that it is his parrot Poll.

Summary: Chapter XVII —
I Improve Myself in the Mechanic Exercises
Wary of sea journeys, Crusoe spends a quiet year in his new home, missing nothing but human contact. He is pleased with his newly developed skills of basket making and pottery making. Alarmed by his low supply of gunpowder and wondering how he will feed himself if unable to shoot goats, Crusoe decides he must learn animal husbandry and tries to catch a small number of goats. He builds a pit in which he traps three young kids, and within a year and a half Crusoe has a flock of twelve goats. He learns to milk them, setting up a dairy that provides him with cheese and butter. He is pleased at his "absolute command" over all the subjects of his island kingdom and enjoys dining like a king surrounded by his parrot, his senile dog, and his two cats. He provides us with a brief inventory of his island holdings: he has two "plantations" on the island, the first his original home or "castle," the second his "country seat." He has a grape arbor, fields under cultivation, and enclosures for his "cattle," or goats.

Analysis: Chapters XIII–XVII
With his survival no longer in question, Crusoe begins to redefine himself not as a poor castaway, but as a successful landowner. We see again how important his attitude is. He begins to refer to his island dwelling as his "home" and his "castle," and when he constructs a shady retreat inland, he calls it his "bower" or "country seat," both references having upper-class connotations. He refers to

the totality of his land as his "plantations" and even refers to his goats as his "cattle." All these terms suggest that his relationship to the island is becoming more proprietary, involving a much greater sense of proud ownership than before, though of course the ownership is a fiction, since there is no deed to this land. Naturally, he still has gloomy moods in which he bemoans his fate and views the island as a prison. But now the alternation between his different moods allows us to see how subjective his situation is and how nearly impossible it is to define Crusoe's island experience objectively. Totally dependent on his frame of mind, it is, as he says, "my reign, or my captivity, which you please."

Crusoe's sad lack of human contact in an otherwise satisfied life is first noted toward the beginning of Chapter XVII, when he remarks that "I thought I lived very happily in all things, except that of society." We can feel how much he misses social relations when he takes the trouble to teach his parrot to talk, though Defoe allows us to imagine how boring their conversations must be, since the parrot can only say Robinson's name and ask where he has come from. Nevertheless, Crusoe calls the bird his "sociable creature," and we are made aware of how starved for company our hero actually is. The same desire for affectionate relations explains his fondness for his new pet goat in Chapter XIV, though we wonder how devoted to it Crusoe can be when he forgets about it for a week and nearly starves it to death. Crusoe's idea of a social gathering presupposes himself at center stage and with the most power, as we see when he describes the dinners he has with his parrot, dog, and cats, where he presides over them all "like a king." Crusoe's eagerness to display superior power in social relations foreshadows his later relationship with his servant Friday.

With the passage of many years on the island by the end of these chapters, Crusoe is beginning to accept his island existence as his life. Accordingly, he is beginning to show a desire to integrate past and present into one totality. Thus, for the first time on the island, Crusoe refers to childhood memories in Chapter XIII, when the subject of basket making leads him to recall the basket weavers in his father's town. He says, "when I was a boy, I used to take great delight in standing at a basket maker's, in the town where my father lived, to see them make their wickerware." The young Crusoe used to lend his hand, so that when as a grown man he again makes baskets, his childhood and adulthood fuse for an instant. The same union of past and present is notable in Crusoe's new interest in his life's calendar repetitions. When he fixates on the fact that he left his father's house the same day he entered slavery, or arrived on the island the same day he was born, he shows a desire to integrate earlier and later parts of his life. No longer just missing the past or living in the present moment, he is trying to bring the two together and see his life as a whole.

CHAPTERS XVIII–XXIII

SUMMARY: CHAPTER XVIII —
I Find the Print of a Man's Naked Foot
Crusoe is astonished one day to discover the single print of a man's naked foot in the sand. Crusoe is terrified and retreats to his "castle," where he entertains thoughts that the devil has visited the island. His conclusion that it is not the devil's but a real man's footprint is equally terrifying, and Crusoe meditates on the irony of being starved for human contact and then frightened of a man. Driven wild by fear, Crusoe fortifies his home and raises guns around it, keeping watch whenever possible. Concerned about his goats, he contrives to dig an underground cave in which to herd them every night and creates another smaller pasture far away to keep a second flock. Crusoe spends two years living in fear.

SUMMARY: CHAPTER XIX —
I See the Shore Spread with Bones
Coming down to a far part of the shore, Crusoe finds the beach spread with the carnage of humans. Eventually realizing that he is in no danger of being found by the cannibals, Crusoe's thoughts turn to killing them as perpetrators of wicked deeds and thereby saving their intended victims. Waiting every day on a hillside fully armed, Crusoe eventually changes his mind, thinking that he has no divine authority to judge humans or to kill. He also realizes that killing them might entail a full-scale invasion by the other savages.

SUMMARY: CHAPTER XX — *I Seldom Go from My Cell*
Crusoe describes the measures he takes to avoid being spotted by the cannibals. He rarely burns fires, removes all traces of his activities when leaving a place, and even devises a way to cook underground. While descending into a large cave he has discovered, he is shocked to see eyes staring at him. Crusoe is frightened and returns with a

firebrand, only to find it is an old he-goat. Crusoe is pleased with this new cave and considers moving into it. Mounting to his lookout spot later, Crusoe spots nine naked savages on the beach, lingering among the remains of their cannibal feast. He proceeds toward them with his gun, but when he arrives they are already out to sea again. Crusoe inspects the human carnage with disgust.

SUMMARY: CHAPTER XXI — *I See the Wreck of a Ship*
On May 16, Crusoe is reading the Bible when he is surprised by a distant gunshot followed closely by another. He senses the shots are coming from a ship and builds a fire to notify the seamen of his presence. By daylight he perceives that the shots have come from the wreck of a ship whose men are now either gone or dead. Once again he thanks Providence for his own survival. Going down to the shore, where he discovers a drowned boy, he prepares to paddle out to the ship in his canoe. He finds the ship is Spanish and contains wine, clothing, and a great treasure in gold bars and doubloons, all of which he hauls back to his dwelling.

SUMMARY: CHAPTER XXII —
I Hear the First Sound of a Man's Voice
Crusoe reflects on the "original sin" of disobeying his father, recounting the foolish decisions he has made throughout his life. One night he dreams that eleven cannibals arrive on his island to kill a victim who escapes and runs to Crusoe for protection. About a year and a half afterward, Crusoe finds five canoes on the island and thirty cannibals on the beach preparing two victims for slaughter. After the first is killed, the second breaks away and runs toward Crusoe's hiding place. He is pursued by two cannibals but is faster than they are. Crusoe attacks both pursuers and persuades the frightened victim to approach. Finding Crusoe friendly, the native vows devotion to his liberator. After burying the remains of the two pursuers so as not to be tracked later, Crusoe and the native return to his camp, where the native sleeps.

SUMMARY: CHAPTER XXIII — *I Call Him Friday*
Crusoe names the native Friday to commemorate the day on which Crusoe saves the native's life. Friday again asserts his subservience to Crusoe. Crusoe teaches him simple English words and clothes him. Returning together to the slaughter scene, Crusoe has Friday clean up the bones and skulls and tries to convey to his servant the

horror of cannibalism. Crusoe is delighted with his new companion and teaches him to eat goat meat instead of human flesh. He realizes he must expand his grain cultivation, which Friday helps him to do.

ANALYSIS: CHAPTERS XVIII–XXIII

Crusoe's discovery of a mysterious single footprint in the sand is one of the most unforgettable and significant events of the novel, since it condenses into one moment Crusoe's contradictory attitude toward other humans: he has been craving human society, yet when it arrives he is deeply afraid of it. Crusoe himself comments on this irony when he says, "How strange a checker-worker of Providence is the life of man! . . . Today we love what tomorrow we hate!" Indeed, he hates this human intruder almost as much as he hates the devil himself, whose footprint he originally suspects it is. It is hard to explain why Crusoe immediately leaps to a negative conclusion about the footprint, why he is sure it is the sign of an enemy rather than a friend. Crusoe's reaction shows how solitude has become his natural state, making any human contact seem unnatural and highly disturbing.

The appearance of Friday is a major development in the novel, which has had only one character in it for a large part. The sweetness and docility of Friday, who is a cannibal, and the extraordinary ease with which Crusoe overcomes Friday's two pursuers, leads us to rethink Crusoe's earlier fear. Crusoe lives in terror of the cannibals for many years, scarcely daring to leave his cave and reduced to a cavemanlike existence. Then, in only a few minutes, he stops two cannibals and makes another his lifelong servant. Suddenly it seems that Crusoe has feared not the savages themselves, but his own exaggerated mental image of them. Thus, Crusoe's self-awareness arises as a major theme of the novel, and Crusoe illustrates that a better understanding of himself and his fears leads him to more prosperity and satisfaction in life. Friday's instantaneous servitude to Crusoe also raises questions about Crusoe's sense of his own rank and power. Crusoe easily could lift Friday from the ground when Friday grovels before him, but he does not. Without so much as a second thought, Crusoe accepts Friday as a servant and an inferior, assuming his own superiority. Friday may be the first New World "savage" in English literature to force a questioning of whether white people should automatically assume superiority over other races.

Crusoe's religious awareness continues to grow in these chapters. Almost every major event is taken either as cause for repentance or as proof of God's mercy. Crusoe's first assumption on seeing the footprint on the beach is that it is a mark of the devil, showing that supernatural or divine explanations have priority over natural ones in his mind. When the gunshots are heard from the wrecked ship, Crusoe is reading the Bible, and when he compares the fate of the shipwrecked men to his own fate, it seems as if he begins to see the whole process as a religious lesson. When Crusoe decides not to open fire on the cannibal feast, he does so out of a religious conviction that he has not the "authority or call . . . to pretend to be judge and executioner upon these men as criminals." Though he later admits there were also practical reasons for not killing them, his religious reason comes across with sincerity. Perhaps most strikingly, in Chapter XXII Crusoe compares his disobedience of his father to Adam and Eve's disobedience of God in Eden, referring to his own "original sin." The Bible, the devil, and God are all becoming very closely entwined in the fabric of Crusoe's everyday life on the island.

CHAPTERS XXIV–XXVII

SUMMARY: CHAPTER XXIV — *We Make Another Canoe*
Crusoe begins to love Friday and, in the course of rudimentary conversations with him, learns that the cannibals periodically visit the island. Crusoe also acquires enough geographical information to locate himself near Trinidad. Crusoe finds out that Friday is aware of mainland Spaniards who kill many men. Crusoe attempts to educate Friday in religious matters and finds that his servant easily understands the notion of God, to whom Friday draws similarities with his own deity Benamuckee. Friday has more difficulty understanding the devil, not grasping why God does not rid the world of this evil being permanently, and Crusoe has trouble answering this question. Crusoe admits that he lacks the religious knowledge necessary for instructing Friday in all the aspects of God and the devil. Friday reports that the cannibals have saved the men from the shipwreck discovered by Crusoe before Friday's liberation and that those men are living safely among the natives now. When Friday expresses a yearning to return to his country, Crusoe fears losing him, and when Crusoe considers trying to join the shipwreck survivors, Friday becomes upset and begs Crusoe not to leave him. Together, the two build a boat in which they plan to sail to Friday's land in November or December.

SUMMARY: CHAPTER XXV —
We March Out Against the Cannibals

> *My island was now peopled, and I thought myself*
> *very rich in subjects . . . how like a king I looked.*
> (See QUOTATIONS, p. 44)

Before Crusoe and Friday have a chance for their voyage to the cannibals' land, the cannibals visit Crusoe's island. Twenty-one natives come in three canoes to carry out another cannibalistic attack on three prisoners. Hesitant on moral grounds to kill so many, Crusoe reasons that since Friday belongs to an enemy nation, the situation can be construed as a state of war in which killing is permissible. Approaching the shore, Crusoe observes that one of the prisoners is a European. Crusoe and Friday fall upon the cannibals and quickly overcome them with their superior weapons, allowing only four to escape. Friday is overjoyed to find that another of the prisoners is his own father. Crusoe and Friday feed the dazed prisoners and carry them back to Crusoe's dwelling, where a tent is erected for them. Crusoe reflects contentedly on the peopling of his kingdom with loyal subjects.

SUMMARY: CHAPTER XXVI —
We Plan a Voyage to the Colonies of America

After conversing with his "two new subjects," Friday's father and the Spaniard, Crusoe revisits his earlier dream of returning to the mainland. Crusoe asks the Spaniard whether he can count on the support of the remaining men held on the cannibals' territory. The Spaniard says yes, but reminds Crusoe that food production would have to be expanded to accommodate so many extra men. With the help of his new workers, Crusoe increases his agricultural capacity. He gives each of the new men a gun.

SUMMARY: CHAPTER XXVII — *We Quell a Mutiny*

One day Friday comes running to Crusoe with news that a boat is approaching the island, and Crusoe, with his spyglass, discovers it to be English. Crusoe is suspicious. Near the shore, Crusoe and Friday discover that the boat contains eleven men, three of whom are bound as prisoners. Friday suspects that the captors are preparing for cannibalism. When the eight free men wander around the island, Crusoe approaches the prisoners, who mistake him for an angel. One prisoner explains that he is the captain of the ship and that the sailors have mutinied. Crusoe proposes that in exchange for liberating him and the other two, he and Friday should be granted free passage to England. The captain agrees and Crusoe gives him a gun. Crusoe realizes that the other seamen may notice something wrong and send more men onshore to overpower Crusoe's men. They disable the boat to prevent the additional men from escaping.

Sure enough, ten seamen come in from the ship to discover the boat destroyed. Leaving three in the second boat as watchmen, the other seven come ashore. Crusoe then sends Friday and another to shout at the men from various directions, and Crusoe succeeds in confusing and tiring them so that they are finally separated. The men in the boat eventually come inland and are overwhelmed by Crusoe's stratagems. On behalf of Crusoe, the captain, finally addressing the remaining men, offers to spare everybody's life except that of the ringleader if they surrender now. All the mutineers surrender. The captain makes up a story that the island is a royal colony and that the governor is preparing to execute the ringleader the next day.

ANALYSIS: CHAPTERS XXIV–XXVII

The affectionate and loyal bond between Crusoe and Friday is a remarkable feature of this early novel. Indeed, it is striking that this tender friendship is depicted in an age when Europeans were engaged in the large-scale devastation of nonwhite populations across the globe. Even to represent a Native American with the individual characterization that Defoe gives Friday, much less as an individual with admirable traits, was an unprecedented move in English literature. But, in accordance with the Eurocentric attitude of the time, Defoe ensures that Friday is not Crusoe's equal in the novel. He is clearly a servant and an inferior in rank, power, and respect. Nevertheless, when Crusoe describes his own "singular satisfaction in the fellow himself," and says, "I began really to love the creature," his emotional attachment seems sincere, even if we object to Crusoe's treatment of Friday as a creature rather than a human being.

As the bond between Crusoe and Friday becomes stronger, the similarities between the two men's cultures gain more importance than their differences. Crusoe is struck by the ease with which Friday learns about the Christian God, finding a close resemblance with the native's own deity Benamuckee. Friday is less able to understand the devil, but it is soon revealed that Crusoe does not understand him perfectly either, when Crusoe admits that he has more "sincerity than knowledge" in the subject of religious instruction. Crusoe first believes the savages to be wicked, but we soon learn that the cannibals have shown an almost Christian charity in saving seventeen European men from the shipwreck. Moreover, Chapter XXVII, with its mutiny and scheduled execution, reminds us that Europeans kill their own kind too, just like Friday's people. The coincidental numerical equivalence between the eleven savages arriving in Crusoe's dream in Chapter XXII and the eleven Europeans now arriving after the mutiny is Defoe's method of emphasizing the similarities between natives and Europeans. Both groups can be violent and murderous, yet both groups can also produce individuals—like Crusoe and Friday—who are kind and good. Generalizing them into the good and the bad, or the civilized and the wild, proves impossible.

Crusoe's story, which has until now been mainly about his own individual survival, takes on a strong political and national dimension when Crusoe wonders whether he can trust the other sixteen Spaniards—who are, historically, often enemies of the British—as his comrades-in-arms against the cannibals. Ironically, it turns out that he can trust these foreigners much more than he can his own countrymen, the eight English mutineers he encounters later. Furthermore, the two non-European cannibal "nations," as Friday terms them, enlarge this national dimension. Friday explains that the cannibals do not eat each other randomly, but that each nation eats only its enemy. Therefore, those cannibalistic actions that seem steeped in savagery are in fact governed by political motives. In Chapter XXV, Crusoe is reluctant to kill the cannibals until he reasons that Friday is in a state of war, thus making murder permissible. This nationalist thinking permeates Crusoe's language too. As usual, our hero's vocabulary reveals much about how he imagines his role on the island, and he starts to describe himself as "generalissimo" of an "army," with Friday as his "lieutenant-general." No longer a mere castaway, Crusoe now openly refers to himself as a national leader of military forces. When he refers to his two new guests on the island as his "subjects," we sense how deeply ingrained his imagined national role as king of the island has become.

Chapters XXVIII–XXXI

SUMMARY & ANALYSIS

SUMMARY: CHAPTER XXVIII — *We Seize the Ship*
Having defeated the mutineers, Crusoe decides that it is time to seize
the ship, and he tells the captain of his plans. The captain agrees.
Crusoe and the captain intimidate the captive mutineers with a fic-
titious report that the island's governor intends to execute them all
but would pardon most of them if they help seize the ship. To guar-
antee the men's promises, Crusoe keeps five hostages. The plan
works: the rebel captain on the ship is killed, and the ship is
reclaimed. When Crusoe glimpses the ship, he nearly faints from
shock. In gratitude, the captain presents Crusoe with gifts of wine,
food, and clothing. The mutineers are offered the chance to remain
on the island in order to avoid certain execution for mutiny in
England. Gratefully, they accept. On December 19, 1686, Crusoe
boards the ship with his money and a few possessions and sets sail
for England after twenty-eight years on the island. Back in England,
Crusoe discovers that the widow who has been guarding his money
is alive but not prosperous. Crusoe's family is dead, except for two
sisters and the children of a brother. Crusoe decides to go to Lisbon
to seek information about his plantations in Brazil.

SUMMARY: CHAPTER XXIX —
I Find My Wealth All About Me

> *It is impossible to express here the flutterings of my*
> *very heart . . . when I found all my wealth about me.*
> (See QUOTATIONS, p. 46)

Arriving in Lisbon, Crusoe looks up his old friend and benefactor,
the Portuguese captain who first took him to Brazil. The Portuguese
captain tells Crusoe that his Brazilian lands have been placed in
trust and have been very profitable. The captain is indebted to Crusoe for a large sum that he partially repays on the spot. Crusoe,
moved by the captain's honesty, returns a portion of the money.
Obtaining a notarized letter, Crusoe is able to transfer his Brazilian
investments back into his own name. He finds himself in possession
of a large fortune. Crusoe sends gifts of money to his widow friend
and to his two sisters. Tempted to move to Brazil, Crusoe decides
against the idea because he is reluctant to become Catholic. He
resolves to return to England, but he is averse to traveling by sea,

removing his baggage from three different ships at the last moment. He later learns that two of those ships are either taken by pirates or foundered. Crusoe decides to proceed on land, assembling a traveling group of Europeans and their servants.

SUMMARY: CHAPTER XXX — *We Cross the Mountains*

Crusoe and his group set out from Lisbon and reach the Spanish town of Pampeluna (Pamplona) in late autumn, and Crusoe finds the cold almost unbearable. The snow is excessive, forcing the group to stay several weeks in Pamplona. On November 15 they finally set out toward France, despite inclement weather. They encounter three wolves and a bear in the woods. Friday kills a wolf and drives away the others. Friday also amuses the group by teasing the bear before killing it. Proceeding onward, the group encounters a frightened horse without a rider, and then finds the remains of two men who have been devoured by wolves. Three hundred wolves soon surround Crusoe's group. The group shoots the wolves and frightens them with an explosion of gunpowder, finally driving them away. Arriving at last in Toulouse, France, Crusoe learns that his group's escape from the wolves was virtually miraculous.

SUMMARY: CHAPTER XXXI — *I Revisit My Island*

Crusoe lands safely at Dover, England, on January 14. He deposits his personal effects with his widow friend, who cares for him well. Crusoe contemplates returning to Lisbon and going from there to Brazil, but he is once again dissuaded by religious concerns. He decides to stay in England, giving orders to sell his investments in Brazil. This sale earns Crusoe the large fortune of 33,000 pieces of eight. Since Crusoe is unattached to any family members and is used to a wandering life, he again thinks about leaving England, though the widow does all she can to dissuade him. Crusoe marries, but after the death of his wife he decides to head for the East Indies as a private trader in 1694. On this voyage he revisits his island. Crusoe finds that the Spaniards who have remained there have subjugated the mutineers, treating them kindly. Crusoe provides them with gifts of cattle, supplies, and even women. The colony has survived a cannibal invasion and is now prospering.

ANALYSIS: CHAPTERS XXVIII–XXXI

The last chapters force us to reevaluate the escape from the island of which Crusoe has spent decades dreaming. It is ironic that he has yearned, plotted, and labored to get off the island, but when he finally does, the return home seems curiously unsatisfying. We might imagine that Europe feels safe and comfortable to him after his ordeal, but the opposite is true: in Spain, Crusoe faces inclement weather, a bear, and 300 ravenous wolves. His island with its bower seems positively luxurious by comparison. Nor does Europe offer Crusoe the human society he has craved as a castaway. The widow and the Portuguese captain are kind, but we feel they do not offer him the love and intense affection Friday shows him. When Crusoe gets married in England, he seems indifferent to his wife, whose name he does not even bother to tell us. In short, with "no family" and "not many relations," and with little interest in forging new relationships, Crusoe appears almost as isolated in England as he does on his island. Defoe thus invites us to wonder whether Crusoe would have been happier if he had remained in his little kingdom forever and makes us question the value of the return to civilization that Crusoe thinks he desires.

The religious dimension of Crusoe's ordeal reaches its climax in his final salvation and reward. Crusoe so easily reclaims his earlier fortune—and, indeed, finds it so immensely multiplied—that the restoration of his possessions seems more like a miraculous windfall—manna from heaven—than mere good luck. We sense that Crusoe imagines God to be rewarding him for his devout patience, especially when he explicitly compares himself to Job: "I might well say now, indeed, that the latter end of Job was better than the beginning." For Crusoe, the shipwreck, the decades of isolation, and the final rescue have not been merely events in a long adventure story, as children read it today, but elements in a religious or moral tale of instruction. Specifically, it is a Protestant tale, with its emphasis on the virtues of independence, self-examination, and hard work. Crusoe underscores this Protestant aspect by mentioning twice that he does not go to Brazil because he would have to convert and live as a Catholic there. Implicitly, Crusoe makes his survival into proof of God's approval of his particular faith.

Crusoe's story is often read in modern times as an allegory of colonialism, and there is much in the last chapters to defend this view. Friday's subjugation to Crusoe reflects colonial race relations, especially in Crusoe's unquestioning belief that he is helping Friday by making him a servant. Moreover, colonial terminology appears. When dealing with the hostile mutineers, Crusoe and the captain intimidate them by referring to a fictional "governor" of the island who will punish them severely. This fiction of a governor foreshadows the very real governor who will no doubt be installed on the island eventually, since Crusoe has apparently claimed the territory for England. The prosperity of the island after Crusoe leaves it is emphasized in the last chapter: it is no longer a wasteland, as when he first arrives, but a thriving community with women and children. This notion of triumphantly bringing the blessings of civilization to a desolate and undeveloped locale was a common theme of European colonial thought. Indeed, Crusoe explicitly refers to this community as "my new colony in the island," which makes us wonder whether he really considers it his *own,* and whether it is officially a colony or merely figuratively so. In any case, Crusoe has turned his story of one man's survival into a political tale replete with its own ideas about imperialism.

Important Quotations Explained

1. "O drug!" said I aloud, "what art thou good for?
    Thou art not worth to me, no, not the taking off of
    the ground; one of those knives is worth all this heap;
    I have no manner of use for thee; e'en remain where
    thou art and go to the bottom as a creature whose life
    is not worth saving." However, upon second
    thoughts, I took it away. . . .

Crusoe's contradictory relationship with money is seen in this affirmation in Chapter VI, when he declares that the gold he discovers is worthless, only moments before hauling it away for safekeeping. He does the same thing many years later, expressing scorn for the treasure on the Spanish wreck, but then taking it to shore. The conflict between spiritual aims (scorning worldly wealth) and material ambitions (hoarding gold) reflects the novel's tension between the practical and the religious. Moreover, Crusoe's combination of disdain and desire for money is also interesting because Crusoe is conscious of his conflicted feelings only in a limited way. He calls money a drug and admits that he is addicted—but he is not interested in the way he fails to practice what he preaches. We see how Defoe's focus in the novel is primarily on the practical rather than the psychological, despite the fascinating aspects of Crusoe's mind. Crusoe's mixed feelings about the gold also reflect his nostalgia for human society, since he tells us that money has no value in itself, unlike the useful knives to which he compares it. It has only a social worth, and thus reminds us that Crusoe may still be a social creature despite his isolation.

2. My island was now peopled, and I thought myself
    very rich in subjects; and it was a merry reflection,
    which I frequently made, how like a king I looked.
    First of all, the whole country was my own mere
    property, Baso that I had an undoubted right of
    dominion. Secondly, my people were perfectly
    subjected. I was absolute lord and lawgiver, they all
    owed their lives to me, and were ready to lay down
    their lives, if there had been occasion of it, for me.

This passage, from Chapter XXV, shows us Crusoe's astonishing
ability throughout the novel to claim possession of things. He sells
his fellow slave Xury to the Portuguese captain even though he has
no claim of ownership over the boy. He seizes the contents of two
wrecked ships and takes Friday as his servant immediately after
meeting him. Most remarkably, he views the island itself as "my
own mere property" over which he has "an undoubted right of
dominion." We may wonder why he has no reason to at least *doubt*
his right of dominion, but his faith in his property rights seems absolute. Moreover, Crusoe's conception of property determines his
understanding of politics. He jokes about his "merry reflection" of
looking like a king, but it seems more than a merry thought when he
refers to "my people" being "perfectly subjected." Kingship is like
ownership for Crusoe. He does not mention any duties or obliga-
tions toward his people. His subjects are for him like his possessions: he imagines them grateful for being owned, expecting
nothing further from Crusoe. Of course, this view is only Crusoe's
presumption. It is hard to believe that the Spaniard sincerely sees
himself as "perfectly subjected" to Crusoe, even if Crusoe does save
his life. Nevertheless, Crusoe's personal point of view dominates the
novel and shows us how deeply colonialism depended on a self-righ-
teous, proprietary way of thinking.

3.   I was born in the year 1632, in the city of York, of a
     good family, though not of that country, my father
     being a foreigner of Bremen who settled first at Hull.
     He got a good estate by merchandise and, leaving off
     his trade, lived afterward at York, from whence he
     had married my mother whose relations were named
     Robinson, a very good family in that country, and
     from whom I was called Robinson Kreutznaer; but by
     the usual corruption of words in England we are
     called, nay, we call ourselves, and write our name
     "Crusoe," and so my companions always called me.

Crusoe's opening words in Chapter I show us the fact-oriented, practical, and unsentimental mind that will carry him through his ordeal. Crusoe introduces his parents objectively through their nationalities, professions, and places of origin and residence. There is no hint of emotional attachment either here or later, when Crusoe leaves his parents forever. In fact, there is no expression of affection whatsoever. The passage also shows that leaving home may be a habit that runs in the family: Crusoe's father was an emigrant, just as Crusoe later becomes when he succumbs to his "rambling" thoughts and leaves England. Crusoe's originally foreign name is an interesting symbol of his emigrant status, especially since it had to be changed to adapt to English understanding. We see that Crusoe has long grasped the notion of adapting to one's environment, and that identities—or at least names—may change when people change places. This name change foreshadows the theme of Crusoe's changing identity on his island, when he teaches Friday that his name is Master.

QUOTATIONS

4. I might well say now indeed, that the latter end of Job
    was better than the beginning. It is impossible to
    express here the flutterings of my very heart when I
    looked over these letters, and especially when I found
    all my wealth about me; for as the Brazil ships come
    all in fleets, the same ships which brought my letters
    brought my goods. . . .

Crusoe's comparison of himself to the biblical character Job in
Chapter XXIX, after his return to England, reveals much about how
he gives his ordeal religious meaning. In Crusoe's mind, his shipwreck and solitude are not random disastrous events but segments
of an elaborate lesson in Christian patience. Like Job, whose faith
was tested by God through the loss of family and wealth, Crusoe is
deprived of his fortune while nevertheless retaining his faith in Providence. This passage also showcases Crusoe's characteristic neutral
tone—the detached, deadpan style in which he narrates even thrilling events. Although he reports that the emotional effects make his
heart flutter, he displays very little emotion in the passage, certainly
not the joy expected of someone who suddenly becomes wealthy.
The biblical grandeur of the original Job is lost in Crusoe's ordinary
and conversational opening, "I might very well say now." We see
how Crusoe is far better suited to plodding and mundane everyday
life than to dramatic sublimity. Even when the events call for drama,
Crusoe seems to do all he can to make them humdrum. This emphasis on the ordinary was a new trend in English literature and is a
major characteristic of the novel, which Defoe helped invent.

5. But no sooner were my eyes open, but I saw my Poll sitting on top of the hedge; and immediately knew that it was he that spoke to me; for just in such bemoaning language I had used to talk to him, and teach him; and he learned it so perfectly that he would sit upon my finger and lay his bill close to my face, and cry, "Poor Robin Crusoe! Where are you? Where have you been? How come you here?" and such things as I had taught him.

When Crusoe returns from his nearly fatal canoe trip in Chapter XVI to find his parrot calling his name, the scene expresses the pathos of having only a bird to welcome him home. Crusoe domesticates the bird in an attempt to provide himself with a substitute family member, as we learn later when he refers to his pets in Chapter XVII as his "family." Poll's friendly address to his master foreshadows Friday's role as conversation partner in Crusoe's life. Crusoe's solitude may not be as satisfying as he lets on. Moreover, Poll's words show a self-pitying side of Crusoe that he never reveals in his narration. Teaching the bird to call him "poor" in a "bemoaning" tone shows that he may feel more like complaining than he admits in his story and that his Christian patience might be wearing thin. Poll's greeting also has a spiritual significance: it comes right after Crusoe's near-death experience in the canoe, and it seems to come from a disembodied speaker, since Crusoe imagines a person must be addressing him. It seems like a mystical moment until the words are revealed not to be God's, but Crusoe's own words repeated by a bird. Cut off from human communication, Crusoe seems cut off from divine communication too—he can only speak to himself.

KEY FACTS

FULL TITLE
The Life and Strange Surprizing Adventures of Robinson Crusoe, of York, Mariner: Who lived Eight and Twenty Years, all alone in an uninhabited Island on the Coast of America, near the Mouth of the Great River of Oroonoque; Having been cast on Shore by Shipwreck, wherein all the Men perished but himself. With An Account how he was at last as strangely deliver'd by Pyrates

AUTHOR
Daniel Defoe

TYPE OF WORK
Novel

GENRE
Adventure story; novel of isolation

LANGUAGE
English

TIME AND PLACE WRITTEN
1719; London, England

DATE OF FIRST PUBLICATION
1719

PUBLISHER
William Taylor

NARRATOR
Robinson Crusoe is both the narrator and main character of the tale.

POINT OF VIEW
Crusoe narrates in both the first and third person, presenting what he observes. Crusoe occasionally describes his feelings, but only when they are overwhelming. Usually he favors a more factual narrative style focused on actions and events.

TONE
Crusoe's tone is mostly detached, meticulous, and objective. He displays little rhetorical grandeur and few poetic or colorful turns of phrase. He generally avoids dramatic storytelling, preferring an inventorylike approach to the facts as they unfold. He very rarely registers his own feelings, or those of other characters, and only does so when those feelings affect a situation directly, such as when he describes the mutineers as tired and confused, indicating that their fatigue allows them to be defeated.

TENSE
Past

SETTING (TIME)
From 1659 to 1694

SETTING (PLACE)
York, England; then London; then Sallee, North Africa; then Brazil; then a deserted island off Trinidad; then England; then Lisbon; then overland from Spain toward England; then England; and finally the island again

PROTAGONIST
Robinson Crusoe

MAJOR CONFLICT
Shipwrecked alone, Crusoe struggles against hardship, privation, loneliness, and cannibals in his attempt to survive on a deserted island.

RISING ACTION
Crusoe disobeys his father and goes out to sea. Crusoe has a profitable first merchant voyage, has fantasies of success in Brazil, and prepares for a slave-gathering expedition.

CLIMAX
Crusoe becomes shipwrecked on an island near Trinidad, forcing him to fend for himself and his basic needs.

FALLING ACTION
Crusoe constructs a shelter, secures a food supply, and accepts his stay on the island as the work of Providence.

KEY FACTS

THEMES
The ambivalence of mastery; the necessity of repentance; the importance of self-awareness

MOTIFS
Counting and measuring; eating; ordeals at sea

SYMBOLS
The footprint; the cross; Crusoe's bower

FORESHADOWING
Crusoe suffers a storm at sea near Yarmouth, foreshadowing his shipwreck years later. Crusoe dreams of cannibals arriving, and later they come to kill Friday. Crusoe invents the idea of a governor of the island to intimidate the mutineers, foreshadowing the actual governor's later arrival.

STUDY QUESTIONS & ESSAY TOPICS

STUDY QUESTIONS

1. *Defoe has his hero practice two different types of writing in the novel. One type is the journal that Crusoe keeps for a few chapters until his ink runs out. The other is the fuller type of storytelling that makes up the bulk of the novel. Both are in the first-person voice, but they produce different effects. Why does Defoe include both types? What does a comparison between them tell us about the overall purpose of the novel?*

With his interest in practical details, Crusoe naturally gravitates toward the journal as a form of writing. His idea of journal keeping follows the example of a captain's logbook rather than a personal diary: it is objective and factual, sometimes tediously so, rather than emotional or self-reflective. But Defoe could not sustain the whole novel as a journal, since much of the moral meaning of the story emerges only retrospectively. Having survived his ordeal, Crusoe can now write his story from the perspective of one remembering past mistakes and judging past behavior. The day-by-day format of the journal is focused on the present rather than the past, and it makes this kind of retrospection difficult. The moral dimension of the novel can best be emphasized through a full autobiographical narrative, with Crusoe looking back upon earlier stages of life and evaluating them.

54 DANIEL DEFOE

2. *Crusoe expresses very little appreciation of beauty in the novel. He describes the valley where he builds his bower as pleasant, recognizes that some of his early attempts at pottery making are unattractive, and acknowledges that Friday is good-looking. But overall, he shows little interest in aesthetics. Is this lack of interest in beauty an important aspect of the character of Crusoe, or of the novel?*

A marked indifference to beauty is indeed an important feature both of Crusoe and of the novel. Not only does Crusoe devote little attention to the visual attractions of his Caribbean landscape, but he also has hardly any interest in more abstract forms of beauty, such as beauty of character or of experience. Beautiful ideas like heroism or moral excellence, for example, rarely enter his head. Moreover, since Crusoe is in many ways a stand-in for the author, we can say that Defoe too seems resistant to aesthetics. This lack of attention to aesthetics is in large part his revolutionary contribution to English literature. Rejecting earlier views that the purpose of art is to embellish and make charming what is ordinary, Crusoe and Defoe show that novels can be profound by focusing on the humdrum, unattractive facts of everyday life that nevertheless are deeply meaningful to us.

3. *Crusoe spends much time on the island devising ways to escape it. But when he finally does escape, his return to Europe is anticlimactic. Nothing he finds there, not even friends or family, is described with the same interest evoked earlier by his fortress or farm. Indeed, at the end of the novel Crusoe returns to the island. Why does Defoe portray the island originally as a place of captivity and then later as a desired destination?*

Crusoe's ordeal is not merely the adventure tale it seems at first, but a moral and religious illustration of the virtues of solitude and self-reliance. At the beginning, Crusoe can only perceive his isolation as a punishment. But after his religious illumination, and after he has turned an uninhabited island into a satisfying piece of real estate, he learns to relish his solitude. His panic at the sight of a footprint shows how he has come to view other humans as threatening invaders of his private realm. His fellow humans in Europe undoubtedly also represent not the advantages of society, but the loss of empowered solitude, and so he dreams of returning to the island where he was king alone.

SUGGESTED ESSAY TOPICS

1. Although he is happy to watch his goat and cat population multiply on his island, Crusoe never expresses any regret for not having a wife or children. He refers to his pets as his family, but never mentions any wish for a real human family. While he is sad that his dog never has a mate, he never seems saddened by his own thirty-five years of bachelor existence. Does Crusoe's indifference to mating and reproduction tell us anything about his view of life, or about the novel?

2. Although Crusoe proudly reports that he allows freedom of religion on his island, giving his Catholic and pagan subjects the right to practice their own faiths, he describes Friday as a Protestant. He attempts to rid his servant of his belief in the pagan god Benamuckee. Why does Crusoe generally show religious tolerance, but insist on Friday's Protestantism?

3. During the return voyage to England from Lisbon at the end of the novel, Crusoe and his traveling party encounter a bear that is frightening until Friday turns it into an amusing spectacle. His teasing of the bear, which prompts the group's laughter, is the first example of live entertainment in the novel. There is no mention of Friday trying to amuse Crusoe on the island. Does this episode foreshadow a new role for Friday after he moves to Europe from the Caribbean? What is Defoe trying to symbolize in having Crusoe bring Friday with him to Europe at all?

4. In many ways Crusoe appears to be the same sort of person at the end of the novel as he is at the beginning. Despite decades of solitude and exile, wars with cannibals, and the subjugation of a mutiny, Crusoe hardly seems to grow or develop. Is Crusoe an unchanging character, or does he change in subtle ways as a result of his ordeal?

5. Crusoe's religious illumination, in which he beholds an angelic figure descending on a flame, ordering him to repent or die, is extremely vivid. Afterward he does repent, and his faith seems sincere. Yet Defoe complicates this religious experience by making us wonder whether it is instead a result of Crusoe's fever, or of the tobacco and rum he has consumed. We wonder whether the vision may be health- or drug-related rather than supernatural and divine. Why does Defoe mix the divine and the medical in this scene? Does he want us to question Crusoe's turn to religion?

REVIEW & RESOURCES

QUIZ

1. When Crusoe eats eggs on the island, from what animal do they come?

   A. Seagull
   B. Quail
   C. Penguin
   D. Turtle

2. Which of the following describes Robinson Crusoe's place in his family?

   A. Oldest son
   B. Middle son
   C. Youngest son
   D. Only son

3. Crusoe names his servant Friday in honor of what?

   A. Good Friday
   B. The day on which the native's life was saved
   C. The last workday before the weekend
   D. The day on which Crusoe's life was saved

4. In what century is *Robinson Crusoe* set?

   A. Sixteenth
   B. Nineteenth
   C. Eighteenth
   D. Seventeenth

5. Where does Crusoe serve as a slave?

   A. North Africa
   B. Sub-Saharan Africa
   C. Spain
   D. Brazil

6. To what does the name Xury refer?

    A. The African port where Crusoe is enslaved
    B. The Brazilian town where Crusoe settles
    C. The name of Friday's father
    D. The name of a slave boy

7. How does Crusoe first grow grain on the island?

    A. Friday gives him seeds
    B. He throws seeds by accident when he discards cornhusks
    C. He salvages seeds from the Spanish wreck
    D. He transplants grain from another area of the island

8. To what does the name Poll refer?

    A. A widow
    B. A pet bird
    C. A servant girl
    D. A ship

9. Of what nationality are the mutineers on the ship that arrives?

    A. Spanish
    B. Brazilian
    C. Moorish
    D. English

10. What does Crusoe do after drinking a rum and tobacco mixture?

    A. Expresses his love to Friday
    B. Paddles his canoe into a dangerous current
    C. Accidentally sets his hut on fire
    D. Experiences a religious illumination

11. Why is Friday excited when he sees the cannibals' captive in the boat?

    A.   The captive is Friday's father
    B.   The captive is Friday's hated enemy
    C.   The captive is Friday's brother
    D.   The captive is Friday's fiancée

12. Crusoe is frightened in a cave when he sees whose eyes?

    A.   A goat's
    B.   A cannibal's
    C.   The Spaniard's
    D.   The captain's

13. Why does Crusoe's first attempt at making a canoe fail?

    A.   The wood is rotten
    B.   The canoe is too fragile
    C.   The canoe is too heavy
    D.   Termites eat through the bottom

14. What livestock makes up Robinson's meat supply on the island?

    A.   Rabbits
    B.   Wildfowl
    C.   Goats
    D.   Cows

15. To what does the name Benamuckee refer?

    A.   Friday's father
    B.   Friday's cannibal feast
    C.   Friday's tribe
    D.   Friday's god

16. Crusoe's father wishes his son to go into which profession?

    A.   Law
    B.   Medicine
    C.   Business
    D.   Farming

17. How does Crusoe impress the natives on the African coast?

    A. Showing them his watch
    B. Killing a leopard
    C. Giving them rum
    D. Sailing the boat in circles

18. The cross that Crusoe erects on the island serves as what?

    A. A religious icon
    B. A scarecrow
    C. A calendar
    D. A sign for passing ships

19. When Crusoe departs on his second trading voyage, with whom does he leaves some of his money?

    A. A widow friend
    B. His father
    C. His sister
    D. A London merchant

20. To what does the name Sallee refer?

    A. Crusoe's first ship
    B. A North African territory
    C. The river bordering Crusoe's plantation
    D. A weapon used by the cannibals

21. In Europe, Crusoe encounters ravenous wolves in which country?

    A. England
    B. France
    C. Belgium
    D. Spain

22. Which type of fruit does Crusoe learn how to dry?

    A. Bananas
    B. Grapes
    C. Pineapples
    D. Apples

23. Two years after discovering the footprint, with what does
    Crusoe find the shore strewn?

    A.   Clothing
    B.   The remains of a ship
    C.   Human body parts
    D.   Goat carcasses

24. After returning to England, what does Crusoe find out
    about his family?

    A.   They are dead except for two sisters
    B.   They are dead except for one brother
    C.   They are not overjoyed to see him alive
    D.   They have moved away from England years earlier

25. Why doesn't Crusoe take his wife back to the island
    with him?

    A.   She is pregnant
    B.   He realizes he does not love her like he loves Friday
    C.   She dies
    D.   She is too prone to seasickness

Answer Key:
1: D; 2: C; 3: B; 4: D; 5: A; 6: D; 7: B; 8: B; 9: D; 10: D;
11: A; 12: A; 13: C; 14: C; 15: D; 16: A; 17: B; 18: C; 19: A;
20: B; 21: D; 22: B; 23: C; 24: A; 25: C

SUGGESTIONS FOR FURTHER READING

BLEWETT, DAVID. *Defoe's Art of Fiction*. Toronto: Toronto University Press, 1979.

BLOOM, HAROLD, ed. *Robinson Crusoe*. New York: Chelsea House Publishers, 1995.

EARLE, PETER. *The World of Defoe*. London: Atheneum, 1977.

FITZGERALD, BRIAN. *Daniel Defoe: A Study in Conflict*. London: Secker and Warburg, 1954.

ROGERS, PAT. *Robinson Crusoe*. London: George Allen and Unwin, 1979.

SCHONHORN, MANUEL. *Defoe's Politics: Parliament, Power, Kingship, and* ROBINSON CRUSOE. New York: Cambridge University Press, 1991.

STARR, GEORGE A. *Defoe and Spiritual Autobiography*. Princeton, New Jersey: Princeton University Press, 1965.

WATT, IAN. *Myths of Modern Individualism*. New York: Cambridge University Press, 1994.

REVIEW & RESOURCES

SPARKNOTES TEST PREPARATION GUIDES

The SparkNotes team figured it was time to cut standardized tests down to size. We've studied the tests for you, so that SparkNotes test prep guides are:

Smarter:
Packed with critical-thinking skills and test-taking strategies that will improve your score.

Better:
Fully up to date, covering all new features of the tests, with study tips on every type of question.

Faster:
Our books cover exactly what you need to know for the test. No more, no less.

SparkNotes Guide to the SAT & PSAT
SparkNotes Guide to the SAT & PSAT—Deluxe Internet Edition
SparkNotes Guide to the ACT
SparkNotes Guide to the ACT—Deluxe Internet Edition
SparkNotes Guide to the SAT II Writing
SparkNotes Guide to the SAT II U.S. History
SparkNotes Guide to the SAT II Math Ic
SparkNotes Guide to the SAT II Math IIc
SparkNotes Guide to the SAT II Biology
SparkNotes Guide to the SAT II Physics

SparkNotes Study Guides in Print: